For CAMILLE C.M.

Many thanks to the staff and children
at Salt Hill Nursery and
Pilgrim's Way County First
for their help and advice.

Copyright © 1996 De Agostini Editions Ltd
Illustrations copyright © 1996 Clare Mackie

All rights reserved.

Edited by Anna McQuinn
Designed by Sarah Godwin and Suzy McGrath

Published in the United States by
De Agostini Editions Ltd, 919 Third Avenue, New York, N Y 10022

Distributed by Stewart, Tabori & Chang,
a division of U.S. Media Holdings, Inc., New York, N Y

ISBN 1-899883-43-6
Library of Congress Catalog Card Number: 96-83068

Printed and bound in Italy

DeA

Crazy Creature Colors

Illustrated by
Clare Mackie

Written by
Hannah Reidy

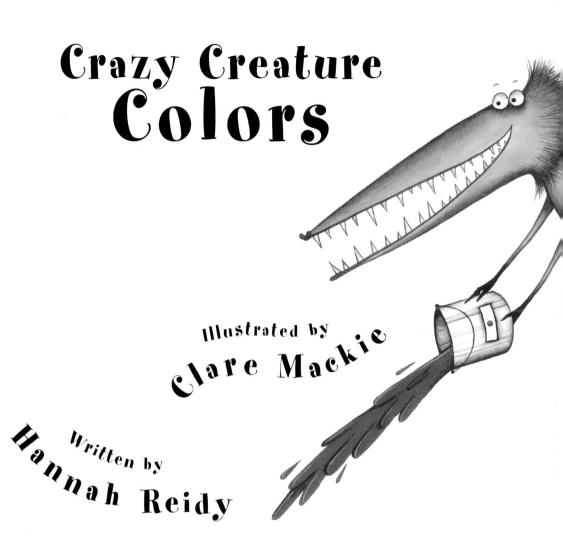

Here's a wall (it is white)
and 3 creatures holding tight
to some paint and some brushes…

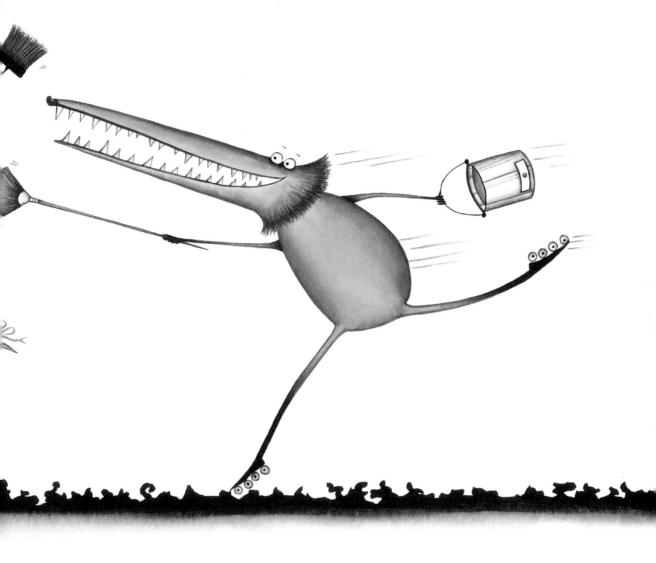

What's next?

The creature who is Blue,
shy and not sure what to do,
paints the low part near the floor part...

Blue!

**The creature who is Yellow,
and a cheerful little fellow,
paints the middle in-between part...**

Yellow!

But a Yellow drip dripped
into the Blue with a dribble,
and mixed a new color in the middle...

Green!

**The creature who is Red,
quickly zooming right ahead,
paints the high part near the top part…**

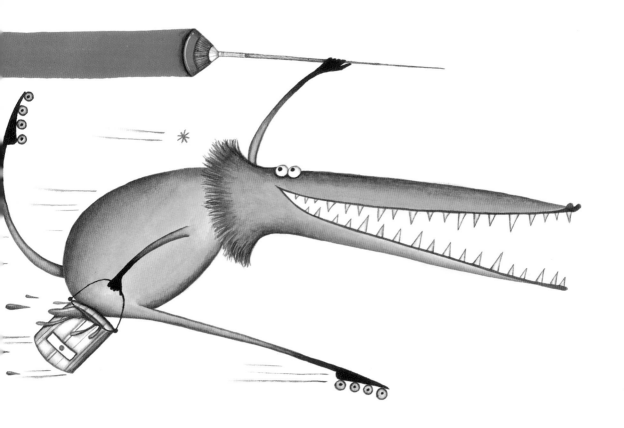

Red!

**But a Red drip dripped
into the Yellow with a dribble
and mixed a new color in the middle...**

Orange!

**Then the Red dripped again,
through the Blue with a dribble,
and mixed another color in the middle...**

Purple!

Until all that was left
was a little bit of white,
"Let's go crazy with the colors!"